"This pamphlet is dedicated to all those who chose to fight back in defence of workers' rights and against the insanity of a system that treats working class people with contempt, jailing those who chose to challenge the bosses' right to throw people on the dole. It is also dedicated to those who supported us, from wives, partners and kids to the local unemployed centres who played such a key role in organising that support. I hope that this shows that it took a lot of courage and soul-searching for those who decided to join the fight, to take the risk in trying to save not just our jobs but the jobs of future generations."

(Lol Duffy, Secretary of the Cammell Laird Occupation Committee, 10 June, 2021)

THE OCCUPATION OF THE CAMMELL LAIRD SHIPYARD IN BIRKENHEAD, 1984

BY JOHN CUNNINGHAM

More publications at workersliberty.org/publications

Contact us or get involved:

workersliberty.org

awl@workersliberty.org

020 7394 8923

20E Tower Workshops
Riley Road
London SE1 3DG

fb.com/workersliberty

twitter.com/workersliberty

instagram.com/workers_liberty

youtube.com/c/WorkersLibertyUK

Printed by Mixam
6 Hercules Way, Leavesden, Watford, WD25 7GS

ISBN: 978-1-909639-55-3

This work is licensed under the Creative Commons Attribution 2.5 Generic License. To view a copy of this license, visit: creativecommons.org/licenses/by/2.5/ or send a letter to Creative Commons, 444 Castro Street, Suite 900, Mountain View, California, 94041, USA.

Cover Image: a group of Cammell Laird workers with the Occupation Committee

CONTENTS

Introduction	5
Shipbuilding in decline: the background to the occupation	7
Organisation of workers in the shipbuilding industry.	9
The situation at Cammell Laird	11
The occupation	15
Workplace occupations.	18
Frank Field: a record of infamy.	21
The aftermath of the occupation	23
Postscripts	25
The roll of honour: the 37 who were arrested and imprisoned.	27
Acknowledgements, sources and references	28
Acknowledgements, sources and references	29

A Cammell Laird worker goes up the rig.

group of Cammell Laird occupiers pose for the camera in 1984.

INTRODUCTION

In 1984 workers at the Cammell Laird shipyard in Birkenhead occupied their workplace in defence of jobs. They started with a strike in June 1984. The strike and the occupation after it lasted just over three months. The occupation was brought to an end on 3 October when the occupiers were arrested. 37 of them were then put on trial, found guilty of contempt of court and sent to prison. Because the action occurred at the same time as the miners' strike of 1984-5, that epic struggle which dominated the news headlines for over a year, it is perhaps easy to overlook it. Workers' Liberty has published this pamphlet so that we can remember.

There are lessons to be learned from what happened. The Cammell Laird 37 have been fighting for years for the convictions against them to be dropped, though sadly some of the men have since died. As the labour and trade union movement struggles to define itself in the wake of the disastrous 2019 election, with the trade union movement in retreat, with the Labour Party headed by an ever rightward retreating Keir Starmer, with sleaze, lies and corruption rampant within the body of political life, it is time to pay heed to that historic exponent of factory occupations – the Italian Marxist Antonio Gramsci, whose ringing words are as true for us today as they were back in 1919: *"It is necessary, with bold spirit and in good conscience, to save civilisation. We must halt the dissolution which corrodes and corrupts the roots of human society. The bare and barren tree can be made green again. Are we not ready?"* This pamphlet aims to be a tribute, a memory, an inspiration and a guide to action for future generations who can – and surely will – learn from this landmark in working class history. From behind prison bars, Lol Duffy, the Secretary of the Lairds Occupation Committee, who was a supporter of *Socialist Organiser* (the forerunner of Workers' Liberty), wrote:

"*We're fighting for jobs, not just for ourselves but for the whole working class community here. If Lairds closes, there's nowhere else to go but the dole. We're proud of what we have done.*" (*Socialist Organiser* 200, 11 October, 1984).

And, in answer to Gramsci's question "Are we not ready?" there has to be only one response – a resounding "yes!"

e Mikasa, flagship of the Japanese Imperial navy, made at the Vickers yard in Barrow, and now on display a military museum in Japan.

SHIPBUILDING IN DECLINE: THE BACKGROUND TO THE OCCUPATION

Few people know about the far away battle of Tsushima Straits in May 1905, between the imperial navies of Japan and Russia. The Japanese blew the Russian ships out of the water, ensuring a resounding victory for this emergent East Asian power and a humiliating defeat for Tsarist Russia (which played its part in the events leading up to the first Russian Revolution of that year). What is rarely acknowledged is that much of the Japanese fleet, modern, fast and with overwhelming firepower, was made in British shipyards (all six of the Japanese battleships, including vice-admiral Tōgō Heihachirō's flagship, the powerful Mikasa, and half the armoured cruisers).

It was the golden era of British shipbuilding, which had long been a key element in British colonial and imperial expansion. The industry dominated the seas, with only Germany and the USA as competitors. In 1900 productivity in British shipyards was twice that of the USA and three times that of Germany. After World War One it was a different story. British yards were slow to adopt some key technical innovations (e.g. the move from riveting to welding) and in many countries indigenous shipbuilding, boosted by the war, continued to expand. Peacetime treaties on limiting naval power also affected the industry. With the onset of the Great Depression in 1929 shipbuilding communities suffered badly: In 1933, 60 per cent of all workers involved in shipbuilding and repair were unemployed; in Scotland the figure was 77 per cent. In those places which relied heavily on shipbuilding the effect was devastating. In the Northeast town of Jarrow it precipitated the famous Jarrow Crusade in October 1936. World War Two and then the Korean War saw a temporary revival of the industry, but the overall trend was downward. In 1956 Japan overtook Britain in terms of production. Now only 23.1 per cent of the world's shipping was built in Britain. In 1957 the huge yards of Harland and Wolff, Vickers, John Brown, Armstrong, Cammell Laird and elsewhere still employed 294,000 workers. That impressive figure hid a disquieting reality.

By the sixties the decline of the industry, particularly relative to its international competitors, was a growing cause for alarm. This was reflected in a flurry of Government reports examining the future of shipbuilding in the UK: the Patten Report of 1962, the Geddes Report of 1966 and the Booz-Allen Report of 1972, all of which recommended various reforms, some of which were incorporated into future Labour government legislation. On 30 April 1975 the Aircraft and Shipbuilding Industries Bill was introduced in Parliament by the then up-and-coming Labour politician Tony Benn, Secretary of State for Industry. A nationalised company was formed, British Shipbuilders. (It adopted the name of the previous owners' association, and the name also was used by the private owners after nationalisation was scrapped).

The law received Royal Assent only in March 1977 due to prolonged resistance by the Conservatives and the owners, who wanted more compensation. Some of them, in a display of perversity rare among even their own class, appealed to the European Court of Human Rights! One of those opposed to the Act was Alfred Robens, at the time the chairman of Vickers and also former chairman of the National Coal Board (NCB). His reign at Hobart House (NCB HQ) had seen the closure of whole sections of the mining industry.

The law provided for the nationalisation of most of the industry. The problems remained. In 1983, under the Tory government of Margaret Thatcher, the yards reverted to private ownership after the passing of the British Shipbuilders Act. This required British Shipbuilders to "privatise its assets". By 1989 the old nationalised British Shipbuilders ceased shipbuilding operations entirely. The saga of contraction and closure continued. The Blackpool Agreement between the Confed (Confederation of Shipbuilding and Engineering Unions) and British Shipbuilders (the owners' organisation, which did not include Harland and Wolff of Belfast) on 24 March 1980, agreed to reduce capacity in the industry to just over 400,000 tons a year.

During the 1950s profits had averaged £120m a year, but a mere £4m had been reinvested while shareholders trousered huge dividends. Capital investment in the industry was half of the national average for manufacturing as a whole. This chronic underinvestment and growing international competition (particularly from Japan and South Korea) meant the industry faced increasing problems. By the early 1960s shipyards had started to close, with the first major closure at William Gray of West Hartlepool in 1962. By 1982, British built ships accounted for just 2.6 per cent of world output. The total workforce in 1984 amounted to 48,000. It continued to fall. By 1990 only 6,000 were employed. Today the Japanese shipbuilding industry, despite having undergone some recent contraction, outstrips the industries of Britain, Germany and the USA combined.

Organisation of workers in the shipbuilding industry.

Shipbuilding by its very nature is a complex business. Every ship (or oil/gas rig) is unique and there are no production lines (as in, for example, the car industry). The main unions involved were the GMB (General, Municipal, Boilermakers), which tended to represent the "unskilled" and semi-skilled workers; the AUEW (Amalgamated Union of Engineering Workers: in 2007 it became part of Unite) covering those who did the outfitting work; the EETPU (Electrical, Electronic, Telecom and Plumbing Union, now part of Unite) covering electrical work; UCATT (Union of Construction and Allied Trades and Technicians, now also part of Unite), covering the many wood fittings (cabin interiors etc.) All unions involved in shipbuilding were part of the CSEU (Confederation of Shipbuilding and Engineering Unions, usually abbreviated to "Confed"). Employment in the industry had historically been precarious. When a ship was finished, workers could be laid off with 24 hours notice or even less, and there might be no work until the next order was placed, so workers tended to guard their jobs, demarcating their boundaries and limits. This occasionally led to friction between different unions and groups of workers, where particular tasks might appear to overlap. In the fifties and sixties management and the media made a great fuss over these "demarcation" or "who does what" disputes, ignoring that this situation arose out of the history of the industry and the lack of employment security, and that similar situations could be found in other industries. Although it provided a handy club with which to beat the workers and their unions, the "who does what" question was little more than a media balloon filled with managerial hot air, utterly peripheral to the many problems faced by the industry.

THE OCCUPATION OF CAMMELL LAIRD SHIPYARD

SHOP CONFED STEWARDS BULLETIN.

ISSUE NUMBER 7.
MAY 1984.

WHO LOST £20,MILLION ?

FACILITIES

* SELF SUFFICIENT WORKSHOPS.
* THREE DRY DOCKS.
* COVERED CONSTRUCTION HALL.
* CADCAM SYSTEM.
* COMPUTERISED PANEL LINE.

PAST RECORDS SHOW

* HMS LIVERPOOL — 12 MONTHS AHEAD OF TIME.
* RFA BAYLEAF — 3 MONTHS AHEAD OF TIME.
* DOME RIG — COULD HAVE BEEN COMPLETED ON TIME HAD IT STAYED IN LAIRDS.
* GAS RIG — WOULD HAVE BEEN FINISHED NOW HAD IT BEEN BUILT IN THE CONSTRUCTION HALL.

WHAT WENT WRONG ?
EXAMPLES OF BAD MANAGEMENT

WHAT PRICE TO:

* CLEAR SILT FROM THE DRY DOCKS?
* PREMATURELY EXTRUDE GAS RIG?
* TRANSFER DOME RIG TO ANGLESEY?
* TRANSFER DOME RIG TO CLYDE?
* TRANSFER DOME RIG TO SWEDEN?
* BUILD THE EMPIRES IN STAFF SECTIONS? (i.e. QA COMMISSIONING PLANNING).

ANSWER ?????   £MILLIONS !!!!!

NET LOSS --- JOBS !

published by Confed Shop Stewards Committee.
printed by volunteers at Birkenhead Unemployed Centre, Argyle Street South.

Stewards' bulletin pointing out management incompetence (May 1984)

The Imperial Russian battleship Chesma on the dock of Cammell Laird, 1916

THE SITUATION AT CAMMELL LAIRD

Cammell Laird was not immune to the processes just described and the yard, established in 1824, prospered and declined in line with the general cyclical trends within the industry nationally and worldwide. For years it was one of the most important shipyards in Britain, building the Mauretania for Cunard, two Ark Royals, HMS Devonshire and RMS Windsor Castle and hundreds of other ships, ferries and later, oil and gas rigs. At its height it employed 12,000 workers. Like other yards around the country Cammell Laird was badly hit by the Depression. Production was boosted by the demands of wartime production between 1939 and 1945, but that provided only a temporary reprieve. By the fifties it was clear the yard was struggling, as were all the other yards in the UK.

After the 1983 British Shipbuilders' Act (scrapping the Labour government's nationalisation) there was a slow but continuous decline in employment. Cammell Laird was de-nationalised in 1985. In 1977 Cammell Laird employed 5,500. By October 1983 this figure had fallen to 3,300. Around the same time management declared 640 jobs were "surplus" and offered voluntary redundancy, which was accepted by 280. Cammell Laird reported losses of £23.8m in 1983. A report in 1984 pointed out that the yard was short of work. Without orders from the navy, Cammell Laird would be in serious trouble. Below are some extracts from the Cammell Laird Confed Shop Stewards' Bulletin no. 3, issued in April 1983 which explains the situation facing the workers in the yard in stark detail.

THE LAST SHIFT

Thursday 14 April could be an historic day in the life-time of Cammell Laird. If Robert Atkinson, chairman of BS, and the Tory government get their way it could be the day the last ship is ever built or launched in this yard.

Everyone will have heard about the proposals by BS to make 9,000 workers redundant throughout the industry and 1,400 of these are supposed to come from Lairds. Although the Blackpool Agreement is officially still in existence there is no guarantee that if there are not enough volunteers it will stop there. Robert Atkinson retires in June and seems determined to destroy this number of jobs either by volunteers or by enforced redundancy which in simple terms means no one's job is safe!

STEWARDS

It was decided at the stewards meeting on 6.4.83 to enlist the support of the local MPs, District and County Councillors. We are also aware that the Mersey and District Emergency Committee of the Confed will be meeting the Company early this week to discuss this most serious situation.

We are under no illusion that MPs etc. can stop these redundancies – stopping redundancies is entirely up to the action of all workers throughout our industry – nevertheless we believe MPs can put pressure on the government to alter course in our favour.

SNC

The SNC will be making a full statement on the April 13 after which there will be a lay delegates conference in late April or early May and after that there will be a full report back to the yards.

ALTERNATIVES

The stewards know there is an alternative to redundancy. We have called on the National Combine Committee to work out a programme of alternative production for the yards. No doubt you have some idea of what can be built in this yard with the wide range of skills available apart from marine-related products – we hope you will pass on your suggestions to us. An alternative does exist if we are prepared to fight for it. It is no use running to the Personnel Department to sell your job for a few pieces of silver. […] While we have a job we must do everything in our power to retain it not just for ourselves but for future generations. […]

[BS = British Shipbuilders, SNC= Shipbuilding National Committee]

Later bulletins listed a range of alternative production around which the yard and its skills could be preserved and revived. "Short term. Scrap and build: This programme would utilise material from scrapped ships in the production of new ships, reducing costs. Factories: Skills already exist within Lairds to build and maintain factory units. The overheads already exist and would not be increased. Council work: Both Liverpool and Merseyside County Council are Labour-controlled and should be sympathetic to saving council and nationalised industry jobs. Plant maintenance: This is already carried out by some other yards (e.g. Smiths Dock/Shell).

"Long term: Undersea exploration. Floating hotels/ accommodation. Pollution monitoring. Wave power. Decompression chambers. Heat pumps. Cement kilns. Recycling equipment. Sugar-beet crushers. Energy production. Oil production platforms. Industrial pipelines. Industrial boilers".

By 1984 the whole of the Merseyside and Wirral area was suffering badly from Thatcherite free-market economics: factory closures, reduced benefits and general economic downturn meant that unemployment and poverty in the region soared. An unemployment rate of 22 per cent was cited but the real figure was almost certainly higher. In the May 1983 council elections, the Labour Party, which locally was heavily influenced by the Militant Tendency, gained 12 seats and took control of the Council from the Tory-Liberal coalition that had previously held sway. Its "frontman" Derek Hatton became a well-known figure in the British media. By the time of the industrial action in Birkenhead, there were two potential centres of resistance to the policies of the Tories: Liverpool City Council resisting cuts, and the miners who had just gone out on a national strike against pit closures in April 1984, and would remain out until early 1985. This volatile background could not but influence the decision made by the workers at Cammell Laird to resist the threat of redundancies. Management at Cammell Laird were making increasing noises about the employment situation in the yard and the threat of redundancies divided the workforce. Here is how Cammell Laird shop steward Lol Duffy reported these developments in the pages of *Socialist Organiser* 184, 21 June.

"Cammell Laird shipyard in Birkenhead is in the process of having half of its workforce made redundant with little reaction from inside or outside the yard. On April 16 a yard mass meeting voted down a resolution from the full-time officials and stewards calling for,

1. No enforced redundancies or closures.

2. A high-powered delegation to parliament.

3. A delegate meeting in support of Cammell Laird involving the local labour movement and community organisations.

4. A mass lobby of Parliament.

Since then the full-time officials have concentrated on trying to motivate support from outside the yard. In the yard, those of us willing to oppose the redundancies are in a minority but are organising our campaign."

Compulsory redundancies were announced on 1 June. The owners threatened to tow away HMS Edinburgh and a gas accommodation rig and finish the work on them in a yard in France. As these two vessels were the only remaining work at the yard, it was imperative that this did not happen. On the 28 June the pickets crossed the Rubicon into the yard, and the strike turned into an occupation.

Eagle-eyed lookouts on the rig keep watch for any police infiltration or other activity detrimental to the occupation.

THE OCCUPATION

The workers occupied the yard in two stages. On 28 June they took over a gas accommodation rig, and on 3 July a navy frigate, HMS Edinburgh. Both were nearing completion, and the occupation pre-empted any attempt by management to tow them away.

The occupation was strengthened by a display of solidarity from tug boat workers and dockers who gave a pledge not to help move the vessels. An Occupation Committee was formed and just over one hundred were involved in the action, almost all of them from the GMB. As a result, 2,000 other workers were laid off. The yard was now, in effect, shut down.

The occupation faced a number of difficulties but the local community and trade unionists on Merseyside and elsewhere were generous in their support. Fresh drinking water was a particular problem, but the occupiers managed. Lookouts were established and speakers went round the country getting the news out and urging support for the occupation. Messages of solidarity poured in from trade union branches around the country, striking miners and Labour Party branches. One of the few voices of dissent – other than the usual suspects such as the media, Tories, the employers and local big-wigs – was the Labour MP for Birkenhead, Frank Field. The local Labour parties disowned him and there were calls, not for the first time, for his resignation. This was not the last time the scab

Field would raise his voice. Unsurprisingly, there were threats of legal action against the occupiers, reflecting the Thatcher government's moves for new anti-union laws to use the law in their war against the trade unions. The employers had at their disposal a range of laws, including trespass. They could seek various court orders and target the main or leading figures in a dispute. There was also an increasing eagerness on the part of the government to deploy large numbers of police to disperse and break through picket lines, as seen in the Stockport Messenger dispute in Warrington and increasingly in the miners' strike. Since the election of Thatcher, employers had demonstrated an increasing inclination to use the law against strikers or those occupying factories, a prime example, again, being the use of court injunctions and the threat of sequestration of union funds in the miners' strike.

A leaflet issued by Merseyside County Council: There was strong local support for the occupation

Here is Lol Duffy, four weeks into the occupation speaking in Ollerton, Nottinghamshire to an audience of striking miners. (From the pages of *Socialist Organiser* 189, 26 July):

> "We're into the fourth week of occupation at the yard now. It started over the management trying to take the two vessels that remain in the yard – a gas rig and a frigate. They're the only work we've got – that's about six months work left on the gas rig and a few months on the frigate. If they take them out of the yard it will be shut – there's no doubt about that. We've got the local tugboat men and the dockers to agree not to handle anything to do with the two vessels. At its peak Cammell Laird employed about 30,000 people and had hundreds of apprentices every year. We're now down to about 1,800. Another 400 redundancies went through this week.
>
> Most of the people in the yard have just accepted the redundancies apart from those who are sitting in – there's about 100 of us at the moment. We've gone down to no apprentices being taken on this year, and about 40 last year. So they have no plans to train any youth in the area in any of the engineering skills – in fact, Cammell Lairds is the last place left in the area that does any sort of heavy engineering.
>
> British Shipbuilders was nationalised in 1977 by the Labour Government.

Since then – and the Labour government started this – there have been 30,000 jobs lost. At the beginning of this year we were going to have a national strike against redundancies. We had a ballot and it was overwhelmingly in favour of a national strike. It was due to start on January 6. The reason why the national officials called the ballot in the first place is that they were used to having ballots go the right way for them, which is not to strike.

We came back to work after the Christmas holidays on the 3rd. Everybody was buzzing. Everybody wanted to have a go. Then on the Thursday they sent the delegates back to the yards, telling them they had got a deal but they shouldn't say anything and shouldn't report back until the official documents arrived a week later. So, effectively, they called the national strike off, just by manoeuvres. So the deal went through. [...]

You've heard about Scott Lithgow. You know what they say about the mines – they're unproductive, you can't get coal out of them. They said the same about Scott Lithgow. They said you can't build ships in a yard like Scott Lithgow – it doesn't have the facilities, the workforce are all lazy. Scott Lithgow was sold off to Trafalgar House. Trafalgar House got a deal when they bought Scott Lithgow, that no other yard in British Shipbuilders would tender against them for any oil-related work. In other words, Cammell Laird was just wiped out by the signing of that agreement on Scott Lithgow.

In British Shipbuilders over the last few years there have been about four or five closures or sell-offs. One of them was Robb Caledon in Dundee. The Shipbuilding Negotiating Committee called a series of one-day strikes over that. We were on strike every Monday for four weeks. It was great for getting over the weekend but it had no effect. Eventually the people at Robb Caledon caved in. Then you had Henry Robb in Leith. There were some people there willing to fight. They approached the Shipbuilding Negotiating Committee for support in line with its stated policy.

The SNC said you don't seem to have much support in the yard. There's only about 15 of you willing to fight, so we can't call action. We can't have all these people losing money for just 15 of you. That's the sort of thing that has been going on – the sort of betrayals we've had from the SNC. At Lairds there were only two major sections ready to fight – the stagers, and my own department, the plant maintenance department.

We're getting massive support from outside Cammell Laird, though a lot of people in the yard have accepted the inevitability of jobs going. [...] We've decided in the occupation that it doesn't matter what they throw at us – whether they throw writs at us or send in the coppers, or whatever – we're not budging. If they do get a writ, we'll have a mass sit-in and call on the people of the area to join us."

Occupiers get comfortable at the GM factory in Flint, Michigan, 1936-37

Workplace occupations.

In the arsenal of working class struggle a factory occupation (or "sit-in", "sit-down", or sometimes "work-in") is a major weapon. In occupying their workplace, workers are not isolated at home or bored or frozen to death on a picket line. The occupied factory can act as a rallying and organising centre and can be a very visible, physical signal to the outside world. Just as important as these considerations is the challenge it poses to ruling class notions of property, ownership and production – the very pillars of the capitalist system. In that respect the "spirit" of occupation is as important as its physical reality.

Occupations have occurred since the time of the Industrial Revolution, but made a greater impact in the twentieth century as factory concentration grew and individual production units developed in size. One of the most famous factory occupations was the wave of seizures that gripped Italy in 1919-20. In Turin alone almost 100,000 workers occupied their factories after being locked out. American car-workers in the great organising drives of the mid-thirties occupied their plants in Flint (General Motors), Detroit (Chrysler, Ford) and elsewhere. Even the mighty Ford combine, once thought invulnerable to unionisation, succumbed, and the UAW (United Automobile Workers) and the CIO (Congress of Industrial Organisations) were born. Interestingly, many of the auto-workers called their action the "Polish tactic". Factory occupations had been effectively employed in Poland and Polish immigrants to the USA caried this memory with them (as indeed did Solidarnosc in 1980s). Paradoxically, US car-worker activists used the more "advanced" tactic of occupation because they thought the less "advanced" tactic of a regular strike would be too difficult to sustain against scabs and cops. There are countless other examples from around the world.

In Britain, the history of class struggle has been punctuated by factory occupations. In some times of more heated conflict they have been fairly common. In 1971 workers at the Upper Clyde Shipbuilders in Glasgow staged a work-in. In 1972 there was a wave of occupation of engineering factories in the Manchester area, and the Fisher-Bendix plant in Kirby was occupied for five weeks. Between 1970-81 there were 264 factory occupations, and of those only 69 were concerned with closure. As the economic situation deteriorated occupations tended to become more defensive, and after 1979, rarer. Between 1979-85 there were an estimated 100 occupations. After that, the number declined and confidence fell in the wake of the miners' defeat. Employers felt more confident and increasingly turned to legal action, particularly using trespass laws and targeting trade union leaderships who became more reluctant to endorse possible illegal action and risk the sequestration of their funds.

Cammell Laird management eventually had a court order issued to remove the occupiers from the yard. They responded by ignoring it. The occupiers stood their ground and a stand-off ensued. Management attempted to influence a section of the workforce who were opposed to the occupation to secure a return to work and a "back to work" meeting was held on 13 August, but the occupation remained solid.

Lol Duffy took up the story of the occupation and the legal threats faced by the occupiers in his report in *Socialist Organiser* 197, 20 September:

"The occupation of the HMS Edinburgh and the gas accommodation rig is now in its thirteenth week. On Thursday 13 September management went back to Manchester High Court for an enactment order on their original writ to have us removed. It was granted. That morning a mass picket of the yard showed the solidarity of the labour movement with the workers in the occupation. Among the pickets were shipyard workers, city councillors, unemployed groups and local MPs."

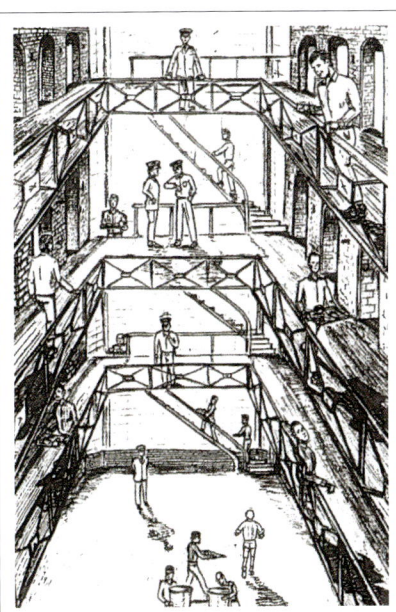

Inside Walton Jail, a sketch by John Dooley, one of the 37.

By 17 September, after many threats, writs were served on the leaders of the occupation committee basically telling them to leave the premises or face arrest. They continued to ignore those injunctions. The occupiers decided not to physically resist the police when they came to make their arrests. The wider balance of forces had shifted. Liverpool City Council had done a deal with the Tory government in July, in fact only a scheme to postpone issues to 1985 (when the Tories would be stronger). The miners' strike had started to go onto the back foot, and would start receding outright by early November. By 11 October *Socialist Organiser* reported: "37 workers from Cammell Laird shipyard have been jailed for a month for fighting for their jobs. 11 were arrested on Monday 1st and another 26 on Wednesday 3rd". In total 37 were now sampling the "delights" of Walton Jail. Walton has a terrible reputation. In 2017 the conditions in the prison were so bad that the governorship had to face a Parliamentary enquiry, and conditions were surely worse in 1984. However, from behind the gloomy walls of Walton the occupiers remained defiant and called on the labour and trade union movement for support.

On 17 October 9,000 GMB members in the City Council went on 24-hour strike to support the jailed 37. However, the response of the official trade union leadership was disappointing, a point made by Lol Duffy (now out of Walton) in *Socialist Organiser* 202 on 25 October,

"It was pretty horrible being in prison, but the attitude of the other prisoners was brilliant. Everywhere we went they shouted out 'You're the lads from Lairds and we're with you ...' I think the local and national officers failed abysmally to mobilise any support for us. They have got a national policy of opposing enforced redundancies. They should have argued from day one of our sit-in – never mind day one of the jailing – for other people to come out in support."

Frank Field: a record of infamy.

There are many words that could be used to describe Frank Field MP for Birkenhead, most of them unsuitable for a publication like this. What follows is just a short run-down on the Labour MP who denounced workers fighting to keep their workplace open, in his own constituency. During the strike and the occupation Field never showed any inclination to meet the workers involved. He was on good terms with high-ranking Tories such as Michael Heseltine and once told him that the strikers were "just a bunch of hotheads." He once described Margaret Thatcher as "a hero" and considered himself one of her confidantes; he was opposed to many social welfare measures; he wanted to reduce time limits on abortion, he was in favour of selling off council houses, supported Brexit, and argued for tighter immigration controls.

Frank Field was first elected as Birkenhead's MP in 1979. He held the position he held until 2019. In the 1987 General Election campaign he denounced Lol Duffy (from the Cammell Laird Occupation Committee), who was the Labour Party candidate in neighbouring Wallasey, and urged a vote for the Conservative Party candidate, Lynda Chalker. After August 2018, when he resigned the Labour whip, he stood as an independent, having just one month previously lost a confidence vote at his Constituency meeting. The tectonic plates of British politics were felt to quake when, in 2019, he formed the Birkenhead Social Justice Party (no, this is not a sketch from Monty Python's Flying Circus, he actually did this!). This mighty political Leviathan came out of the 2019 General Election with a staggering 7,285 votes. The winning candidate, Labour's Mick Whitley, polled 24,990 votes and Frank Field was, thankfully, history. For services rendered to the cause of the ruling class he was made Baron Field of Birkenhead on 11 September 2020. Good riddance!

THE OCCUPATION OF CAMMELL LAIRD SHIPYARD

SHOP CONFED STEWARDS BULLETIN.

ISSUE NUMBER 8.
MAY 84.

WHY SHOULD'NT I TAKE REDUNDANCY ?

IT'S MY JOB !

Over 150 years Cammell Laird built up a workforce of 12,000 for generations of workers.

Since the 1960's they have made over 8,000 people redundant – these jobs will not be replaced.

Lairds plan a further 1,650 redundancies and any future work will be on the basis of casual hire and fire, as in the 1930's.

I'LL BE BETTER OFF FINANCIALLY.

Some people may be tempted by the initial enticement of redundancy payments in order to pay off debts or take that well earned holiday.

However the DHSS state that before a person qualifies for social security the DHSS must be convinced redundancy payments have been used for acceptable purposes – holidays and mortgage payments are not classed as acceptable.

PROSPECTS OF EMPLOYMENT ELSEWHERE.

Employed in 1976 = 23 million.
Employed in 1983 = 17 million.

Unemployment on Merseyside is 29%.
There are only a handful of job vacancies.

24,000 businesses went bankrupt since 1982 – most of them in the engineering and manufacturing industry.

Graduates have to take unskilled jobs.

DON'T SELL THEIR JOBS.

published by **Confed** Shop Stewards **Committee**.
printed by **volunteers** at Birkenhead **Unemployed** Centre, **Argyle Street** South.

The shop stewards' response to offers of redundancy payments (May 1984)

e Sir David Attenborough in dry dock at Cammel Laird, 2019. bit.ly/attenboat

THE AFTERMATH OF THE OCCUPATION

Released from Walton Jail (eleven on 11 October, and the rest on 23 October), the former occupiers continued their campaign to prevent the yard's closures and campaigned for their reinstatement. A picket was maintained and the Strike Committee resumed its meetings on Saturday 17 November. The Committee:

"…decided to step up the fight to win back the jobs of the 43 workers [this includes six who weren't jailed] fighting for the right to work. A mass picket was called for the Wednesday 21 November, the date of a high tide high enough to launch the gas accommodation rig … The Strike Committee also contacted the Shop Stewards' Committees in all British Shipbuilders' yards to ask that they call mass meetings to allow us to address them and call for support in the form of action in line with national lay delegate conference and union decisions to oppose enforced redundancies with strike action and occupations". (Socialist Organiser 206, 1 November 1984)

Despite support from wide layers of the labour and trade union movement, the activities of scabs, supported and encouraged by management, and the reluctance of the trade union leadership to throw its weight behind the strike and occupation, meant that the occupation went down to defeat. Those who refused to support the occupation may have seen themselves vindicated as HMS

Edinburgh and the gas accommodation rig headed for the high seas, but there was to be no plain sailing for Cammell Laird as the yard lurched from one crisis to another. According to no less an authority than MP for Wallasey Angela Eagle (speaking in the House of Commons, 14 Dec 1992) the yard was bought by Vickers Shipbuilding and Engineering Limited (VSEL) in 1986 for the princely sum of £1 (that is ONE pound!). As VSEL already had a yard in Barrow this appeared to be little more than an asset-stripping exercise.

The yard closed with the loss of 900 jobs in 1993 but then spluttered back into life with various mergers, buy-outs and re-brandings, not concerned with re-establishing shipbuilding but with repair work, small-scale projects, and asset-stripping. There have been so many changes of ownership and plans put forward (including one to put the yard into a Community Trust) that it is difficult to follow the myriad twists and turns. *The Guardian* (online), 18 August 2001, reported that, "Hundreds of workers at Cammell Lairds on Tyneside and Merseyside are almost certain to lose their jobs after the company was sold to a repair and conversion company A & P Acquisitions for an undisclosed sum". In the early months of 2006, the company was sold lock, stock and barrel, to private investors. They continued to use the name Cammell Laird for a time but it was renamed Gibdock (Gib = Gibraltar) on 7 December 2009.

Although a Cammell Laird shipyard (the name was re-adopted) still exists in Birkenhead, it limps along. The yard that in 1938 built the Mauretania, the biggest ship ever launched in England at the time, now gets excited about the prospect of building the new Royal Yacht (which isn't a Royal Yacht but some kind of business-ambassador vessel). Even the much-trumpeted polar exploration vessel, the Sir David Attenborough, was not completed without problems. Let's ignore the amusing "controversy" over whether the vessel should have been named "Boaty McBoatface". With a £200m budget the final construction incurred £37.4m losses, an impairment charge of £15.8m (compensation for loss of "goodwill" e.g. name brand recognition or reputation), and was two years behind schedule. It was finally launched on 14 July 2018.

With apparently no sense of irony, the *Liverpool Echo* (3 May 2021) reported that Boris Johnson "…has an exciting vision for shipbuilding in this country and is committed to making the UK a shipbuilding power.[1]" *About 45 days before Johnson's "exciting vision" was announced, Lairds management made 178 workers redundant.*

---

1   ***A shipbuilding power?*** The following was highlighted by the authors of the report National Shipbuilding Strategy: The Future of Naval Shipbuilding in the UK (Ministry of Defence, 2017): *"It is only by building ships again that we will **once again** become good at building ships."* Who would have thought!

die Marnell (on the left) with Billy Albertina

POSTSCRIPTS

It is rare in the kind of situation just described that at a certain point the blinds are pulled down and everyone gets back to their "normal life" (whatever that might mean). Eddie Marnell, a member of the Occupation Committee who became a GMB official, has campaigned for many years for the arrested men and to have their sentences revoked and wiped off the record. Obstructions have constantly been thrown up by various authorities and he has frequently been denied access to documents and records. It has been a long and often frustrating fight. After many years he achieved his first success when, in December 2014, the European Parliament Petitions Committee heard him put the case for the 37 and they responded by calling on the British government to apologise to them. Readers will no doubt be shocked to learn that no apology was forthcoming. Interviewed by Lisa Worth for the online *Nerve Magazine*, Eddie said,

"I want a pardon for all of us skilled men who just fought for our rights. Men stripped of pensions and redundancy just because they stood up for themselves. Men like Tommy Webb, who served on the Atlantic convoys during World War Two. Honest hard-working men who deserved better. And I will go on for as long as I can."

Lol Duffy went on to stand as Labour Party candidate for Wallasey in the 1987 General Election, almost beating the sitting MP Tory Lynda Chalker, turning her previous majority of 6,708 (in 1983) into a mere 279. If it had not been for intervention in the local press by Frank Field, who urged the people of Wallasey to cast their vote for Chalker, then Lol might have won. The Labour Party machinery made sure that there was no possibility of a repetition. Duffy was barred by the National Executive Committee (NEC) from standing again. Of course, no action was taken against Field. The next step by the NEC was to "parachute" Angela Eagle into Wallasey. Despite receiving only a handful of nominations from the constituency she was chosen as the Wallasey candidate to fight the next election, which came in 1992. The skulduggery involved in shoehorning Eagle into her position clearly went against the wishes of the overwhelming majority of the membership.

The occupation and the memories it evokes has never gone away. The premiere of *The Truth*, a play about the occupation by Mike Howl, opened to great acclaim at the Casa Theatre in Liverpool in September 2018. The Justice for Cammell Lairds Campaign has an informative video which can be easily accessed online via the GMB website: https://vimeo.com/382380702. The Birkenhead Labour MP, Mick Whitley, a former trade unionist at Vauxhall's Ellesmere Port plant, was an active supporter of the Cammell Laird occupation and strike. He is currently campaigning for justice for the 37 and will continue to do so until they get it. A House of Commons Early Day Motion, calling for the convictions to be dropped and an enquiry into the events surrounding the occupation, was tabled on 19 April 2021 and was signed by 34 MPs.

There is probably a need for one final word. There is no denying that ultimately the occupation was defeated. The 43 have never been able to get their jobs back, and pensions have been lost. To pretend otherwise is just wishful thinking. Given the employment situation in the Wirral it must have been hard to find fresh employment, and it would have been very unusual for some kind of blacklist (unofficial or otherwise) not to be in operation. Yet can such things be decided on a simple black or white notion of "victory" or "defeat"? There is something called history and there is something tangible and real, which is "class spirit" or "class consciousness", which a month in Walton Jail cannot crush. These are not clichés. They exist because of real social conditions in which men and women live. History is not a closed book. We learn from the past, live it in the present and use it to build for the future.

Karl Marx once famously wrote that, "People make their own history, but they do not make it as they please…" To go on strike and then occupy your place of work at a time when the industry you are part of has been in more-or-less continual decline, and resistance has been at best sporadic, was hardly ideal. But the spirit, class consciousness, however it is labelled or voiced, did not allow for surrender, simply lying down and being crushed. If we look at in this way, then the idea of defeat/victory becomes less tangible. If this is not too mind-bending it was both at the same time.

In 1988 there was a victory for Julie Hayward, a canteen cook at Cammell Laird who took her claim for wage discrimination to the Appeal Court and in a landmark ruling won her case. Cammell Laird workers were on strike again in November 2018, essentially fighting the same battle, against job cuts, as before, and with some limited success. History has not closed its book.

> **The roll of honour: the 37 who were arrested and imprisoned.**
> Eddie Marnell, Michael Byrne, Tommy Webb, Jimmy McCarthy, Joe Flynn, George Whittaker, Francis Roach, Anthony McGarry, John Dooley, Michael Mooney, Colin Early, Thomas Culshaw, Chris Whitley, Tommy Wilson, Lol Duffy, Barry Golding, Aiden Morley, Jimmy Barton, Thomas Cassidy, Alan Prior, John Brady, Andrew Frazer, Philip McKeown, Nicholas Fenlan, Paul Hennessey, John Wright, James Morley, Edward Kenny, Christopher Bilsborough, Christopher Thompson, Stephen Smith, Paul Little, and Jimmy, Billy, Francis, John and Eddie Albertina. (List originally published in the *Morning Star*, 9 October 1984)

Reunion: Lol Duffy is on the right (jacketless).

Acknowledgements, sources and references

Many thanks to Lol Duffy, who wishes it to be known that some of the material used in the research for this pamphlet came from John Dooley and Billy Albertina, as well as much from him. Thanks also to Mark Hoskisson and Mick Whitley MP. Much of the factual and statistical data for this pamphlet has been gleaned from the following: Information accompanying the British Film Institute DVD collection on Shipbuilding, "Exploring the history of the shipbuilding on film"; "From workplace occupation to mass imprisonment: the 1984 strike at Cammell Laird shipbuilders" by Stephen Mustchin in Historical Studies in Industrial Relations No. 31/31 (2011) pages 31-61; The Wirral Archives (part of the National Archives). All are available online and the Early Day Motion mentioned in the text can be found at: https://parliament.uk/early-day-motion/58384. Lol Duffy generously sent copies of his collection of documents, photos and memorabilia of the strike and occupation, and those proved invaluable. The words of Antonio Gramsci are often quoted and were first written by him in the pages of his revolutionary newspaper *Ordine Nuovo* (New Order) 15 May 1919. Gramsci and the factory occupations in Italy are discussed in Paolo Spriano's *The Occupation of the Factories* and Gwyn A. Williams' *Proletarian Order*, both published by Pluto Press in 1975 but now out of print. The thrilling story of the US autoworkers' sit-ins in the 1930s is told in *Labor's Giant Step* by Art Preis, first published by Pathfinder Press in 1964. Lisa Worth's interview with Eddie Marnell can be found in *Nerve Magazine* (online), 16 April, 2018: www.catalystmedia.org.uk. Lol Duffy's election campaign in 1987 is discussed in-depth in How to *Fight Elections: The Story of Labour's Socialist Campaign in Wallasey, 1987*, a pamphlet re-issued by Workers' Liberty in 2016.